D1269519

Illustrated by R O B E R T   M A C   L E A N

Amateur Sugar Maker

BY NOEL PERRIN

**Published for Dartmouth College
by University Press of New England
Hanover and London**

University Press of New England

Brandeis University
Brown University
Clark University
University of Connecticut
Dartmouth College

University of New Hampshire
University of Rhode Island
Tufts University
University of Vermont

Printed in the United States of America

Library of Congress Cataloging-in-Publication Data

Perrin, Noel.
Amateur sugar maker.

Originally published: 1972.
1. Maple sugar.   2. Maple syrup.   3. Country life—
Vermont.   I. Title.
[TP395.P47   1986]   641.3'36   86–5592
ISBN 0–87451–379–0 (pbk.)

The first section originally appeared as
the article "Letter From Vermont"
© 1970 *The New Yorker Magazine, Inc.*
The fourth section, "Steam Coming Out the Vent,"
first appeared in *Vermont Life* Magazine © 1972.

for those lovers of maple sap,
LILY *and* MARGARET PERRIN

Note

THIS BOOK is about building a sugarhouse and making maple syrup in a small Vermont town. It is written in conscious admiration of Henry David Thoreau—not that Thoreau ever did any sugaring. But Thoreau liked to see how little money it is possible to spend, and still do what you want. And he liked to see how much of a project one man can do alone, with just his hands and a few tools.

Having gone to Vermont as a teacher ten years ago, I wanted to try my hand at sugaring. I didn't hope to make my living at it, but I didn't mean just to play games, either. Insofar as possible, I meant to do the work myself, and I meant to keep expenses down to the point where I really would earn a small part of my living by making syrup, as I earn another small part by cutting and selling firewood. I like an edge of hard labor to my life.

Vermont has a long history of people who like that sort of edge. There have been times in its history when almost literally no one in the state wasn't doing the plainest sort of manual work. Maybe not as a career, but sometimes. My favorite example comes from the year 1860. There was then in St. Johnsbury a young man named Edward Fairbanks, a member of the leading family in town and one of the two or three top families in the state. They owned what is now the Fairbanks Morse Division of Colt Industries and was then just the Fairbanks Company. Edward's uncle Erastus Fairbanks was a past governor of Vermont

—and was running again that very fall on the Republican ticket. (He won handily.) Edward himself had gone to Andover and then to Yale, where he graduated in 1859. In 1860 he was home for a year, helping round the factory.

St. Johnsbury, along with about fifty other Vermont towns, was due to be included in the first volume of the *Vermont Historical Gazetteer* that year; and doubtless because of his Ivy League training in scholarship, young Edward Fairbanks was asked to do the history of his home town.

This led him to write to an old farmer in western Vermont named Henry Stevens, the biggest collector of historical documents in the state. He later founded the Vermont Historical Society. Stevens was then sixty-eight, a semiretired farmer who also owned a couple of mills and had served in the state legislature. He had made enough money to send his own son to Yale. And on the side he had picked up about twenty thousand old documents: letters of St. John de Crèvecoeur (for whom St. Johnsbury is named), and so forth.

When Edward Fairbanks wrote and asked if he could come pay a visit and look through the collection, Stevens wrote back:

Burlington, Oct. 10, 1860

Dear Sir: Your letter of Oct. 2 received. In answer to a portion of it as to making a visit here to copy MSS. I have to say—Mrs. Stevens and myself occupy a comfortable house. I have to say further that all who are disposed to make us a call are welcome. We will set the table in the front room 3 days. After that time we dine in the kitchen. Three days we call a visit. According to established usage, if our friends stay more than 3 days it is expected they will do chores night and morning. We find the frock or apron as required. Come when you please. Now as to historical matters. . . .

And Fairbanks, describing the visit years later, said, "I accepted the conditions, was very cordially received; ordered my frock and milking stool at the date specified; stayed more than three days; made lasting friendship with the antiquary."

Into this tradition, which in the end is not of Vermont, but simply American, I like to think of my sugarhouse and my modest output of maple syrup as fitting.

Thetford Center, Vermont
February 1971

The Sugarhouse

THOREAU BUILT HIS CABIN on Walden Pond for $28.12½—a price regarded even in 1845 as low. As he triumphantly pointed out, the mere rent for a dormitory room at Harvard that year was $30.00. In terms of current building costs, his feat seems almost incredible. A common rule for estimating the cost of one-story houses now is to figure $20.00 per square foot of floor space. Thoreau's place was ten feet by fifteen, a hundred and fifty square feet. Built now, it would therefore cost $3,000. It's true that 1972 estimates are heavily influenced by plumbing and electricity, neither of which Thoreau was troubled with. On the other hand, *his* costs included a fireplace, a chimney (he had to buy a thousand bricks and haul a ton of stones for them), and solid plaster walls. Fireplaces and real plaster are regarded as luxuries too expensive for the majority of modern houses.

In the spring of 1969, I set out to build a house in Thetford, Vermont, about the size of Thoreau's down in Massachusetts. Without in the least intending to when I started, I gradually got into a price war with him. He won, of course. Building supplies were so very much cheaper in 1845. Those thousand bricks, for example, he bought secondhand, with the mortar still on them. They cost him four-tenths of a cent each, $4.00 for the whole thousand. That's a very nice price. I, too, have on occasion bought secondhand bricks (besides getting 412 free ones when they tore down the old part of the Hanover Inn in Hanover, New Hampshire, a few years ago). The absolute lowest one can pay for used bricks around Thetford, even bricks caked an inch thick with old mortar, is three cents apiece—$30.00 a thousand. Again, Thoreau's total cost for lumber was $8.03½. Nowadays it is possible to spend that much on four or five boards. But I gave him some stiff competition.

Thoreau and I started equal in that neither of us had to pay anything for land. He built on an eleven-acre woodlot lent him by Ralph Waldo Emerson. (Emerson had picked it up a year earlier for $88.88.) I built in a patch of woods that I already owned. It came, thrown into the bargain, when I bought a brick farmhouse and twenty-five acres across the road for $16,500, back in 1963.

We started unequal in that our purposes were different. Thoreau meant actually to live in his house, and did so for two years, after which a Scot named Hugh Whelan moved in. I *could* live in mine, and find it so snug that I am sometimes tempted to. I actually built it, however, to be a sugarhouse—that is, a place for boiling down maple sap into syrup. I naturally don't have plaster walls. People who make maple syrup in their kitchens often find the wallpaper sliding gently to the floor, and sometimes the plaster itself beginning to crumble. No fireplace, either. But then I have a much grander roof. Thoreau's was an ordinary two-sided affair, such as you see on half the houses in America. Every decent sugarhouse, however, has a steam vent, which is a sort of cupola gone earnest. It rises a couple of feet above the main roof on special small rafters, and it has hinged sides that you open when you start boiling and close again when it begins to snow. Steam vents are hard work. I figure mine balances Thoreau's plaster, and I leave him ahead on the chimney and the fireplace.

Having borrowed Emerson's land, Thoreau picked his house site in late March of 1845. He chose a low hillside about two hundred feet from the shore of Walden. He then borrowed an axe from Louisa May Alcott's father, cleared the brush, and went on to fell twenty or thirty of Emerson's young white pines. This was no loss to Emerson; a stand of pine benefits from thinning. The first two weeks of April he spent gradually hewing them into house timbers. The biggest ones, he says in *Walden,* he hewed six by six—that is, into beams six inches square in cross section. These were for corner posts. He also cut out rafters and studs and plate and sills, "all with my narrow axe." Hand-hewn timbers now often sell for a dollar a foot. Thoreau-hewn ones might fetch a good deal more. But Thoreau himself had not spent a cent.

I picked my site on June 18, 1969. It's about a hundred feet from the Pompanoosuc River, just where a dirt road crosses a small brook (which I plan to use for washing sap buckets). I then got my chain saw and felled two white birches, a wild cherry, a red maple, and about twenty alders, and cut and stacked the wood for use when I start boiling. All this took about three hours. I now had a clearing fifteen feet by twenty, sloping considerably downhill toward the brook. I first planned to hire a bulldozer to level it. But the cheapest you can get bulldozing done in this part of Vermont is $10 an hour, with a minimum charge for two hours, and usually a travel fee besides, so instead I used a shovel and an axe. Leveling took the rest of June eighteenth and the morning of the nineteenth. It left me a little stiff, but financially almost even with Thoreau. So far, I had spent approximately ten cents for gas for the chain saw. To be fair, maybe I should add fifty cents for wear and depreciation.

Timbers put me well behind. "Arrowy" white pines, such as Thoreau used, are hard to come by now, the white pine weevil having grown steadily more ravenous for the past century. I am also not his match with an axe. Few middle-class Americans raised in the suburbs are. Without even much shame, I went to a small lumberyard about two miles away and bought timbers. The yard is owned by a man named Ken Bragg, who does his own logging in the woods, trucks what he cuts, saws it, on occasion planes it, and, finally, is in the retail lumber business. He is usually a hard man to catch. But on the morning of June twenty-first, when I came poking up the dirt road his mill is slightly beyond the end of, he happened to be there, sawing twelve-by-twelve bridge timbers for the town of Strafford, Vermont. More accurately, he was propelling hemlock butt logs down toward the saw carriage with a peavey while Mr. Lewis P. Farwell, his white-bearded, ninety-one-year-old sawmaster, did the actual sawing.

Ken was willing enough to stop and sell me four-by-fours. The fact that he didn't have any was no problem at all. He simply began skipping small hemlock logs over the big ones lined up waiting to become bridge timbers, and Mr. Farwell sawed out my corner posts and sills on the spot. I meanwhile loaded my truck with two-by-fours from a big stack below the mill. Ken dislikes bookkeeping, and quoted a price of eight cents a foot for the whole order. Since I stopped at the village store in Thetford Center on the way home and bought fifteen pounds of nails, my expenses so far totalled:

Site preparation	$ 0.60
280 feet of hemlock 2 x 4 at 8¢ a foot	22.40
80 feet of hemlock 4 x 4, also at 8¢	6.40
Nails, 15 pounds at 20¢	3.00
	$32.40

Thoreau's totalled:

Site preparation	$ 0.00
Timbers	0.00
	$ 0.00

He began spending money immediately afterward, however. Unless you're going to peg everything, you simply cannot build a house without nails. Thoreau did not learn blacksmithing and make his own. He bought them at a hardware store. Nails are the one building material about as expensive in 1845 as now, and his supply set him back $3.90. Nor was this his only cost. Before he started actually building, he also bought his thousand bricks; he bought two casks of lime, for $1.20 each, to make mortar with; and he paid $1.20 to have all this hauled out to Walden. So he was soon out of pocket $11.70.

Each of us framed up his house alone. I suspect Thoreau got his done faster, even though it was bigger. (My sugarhouse is eight feet by eleven.) He had mortised and tenoned all his timbers while he was hewing them out, and he just had to fit them together and spike them. I was two full days with a handsaw cutting mine up, and most of a third day nailing them together. At this point, we each had a skeleton house, a trim rectangular outline with no trace yet of a roof. I don't know what Thoreau used for foundations, but mine consist of four large and six smaller rocks. I got them from a place where I'm making a barway through a stone wall, and they cost nothing.

The next step in housebuilding is the hardest. This is the so-called raising, where you climb up on the skeleton and teeter in the air putting on the rafters. Thoreau, who apparently spent the last two weeks of April bird-watching, with a couple of hours out to dig his cellar and one day devoted to buying boards, raised his at the beginning of May. He asked some friends to help him —"rather to improve so good an occasion for neighborliness," he says in *Walden,* "than from any necessity." I, too, sought help, and in my case it *was* from necessity. Without one to hold and another to nail, I don't quite see how anyone raises a roof. Thoreau did see, and I honor him for it. But I don't admit total inferiority. Modern scholarship has determined that there were no fewer than nine assistant roofers present at Walden: Emerson, Bronson Alcott (who probably wanted his axe back), William Ellery Channing, the two Curtis brothers, Burrill and George, and a Concord farmer named Edmund Hosmer, with his three sons, John, Edmund, Jr., and Andrew. That seems to me excessive and unhermitlike. I got my roof up with the aid of one neighbor, a young Oberlin graduate named Dick Cooper.

Neither Thoreau nor I had labor costs. It would have been absurd for him to pay Emerson —who doubtless let the Hosmer boys do the teetering anyway—and though Dick Cooper will, and sometimes does, work for money, he much prefers to trade labor. So do I, for that matter. He spent a day working on my house; I spent a day helping him cut dead elms for firewood. Dick and his wife and baby have a five-room house they heat with a wood-burning furnace.

Once the roof is raised, you start boarding. Thoreau had his boards already there and stacked. He knew an Irish railroad worker named James Collins, who had moved away from Concord that April, leaving behind a shanty. Thoreau bought all rights to it for $4.25. He should have got some free nails along with the boards, but he says another Irishman, named Seeley, kept pocketing the straight ones, each time he was off carrying a load of boards to Walden.

Thoreau apparently got about three-quarters of the way with what he took from the shanty, and then had to rush to the lumberyard. At any rate, he records an expenditure of $3.78½ for more boards, presumably new ones. I had hoped to use a lot of old boards I found in the barn basement when I bought my farm, but it soon turned out that they had been thrown down there because they were too rotten to use. All I could salvage from a disorderly heap of at least a hundred was enough boards for one side of the roof, and I wish now I hadn't done that. So at the beginning of July I drove up to Ken Bragg's again. (There's no phone at the mill; you just take your chances.) Not finding him there, I drove on to Snelling's lumberyard, in East Thetford. This is a much larger operation, though there's still no sign or any other hint to the public that you can actually buy lumber there. People are always around. Mr. Snelling sold me two hundred feet of wide-board hemlock for $19.00—a good price. Later, I went back and spent another $9.50 for a hundred feet more. Later still, I blew $2.00 on eight feet of white pine to board the sides of the steam vent, which I want fancy. All this sent my expenses soaring up to $62.90 while Thoreau's only crept up to $19.73½.

But after we had boarded our houses, our building methods began to diverge widely, and to my advantage. Thoreau promptly moved into his house, and then he not only plastered it ($1.25 for laths and thirty-one cents for hair to mix in the plaster) but completely shingled the outside, like a Cape Cod cottage, using what he called "refuse shingles." These I take to be what are now called seconds. This elegance cost him $4.00 more.

My walls, on the other hand, were done. Inch-thick hemlock will last indefinitely, and as for the narrow cracks between the boards, in a sugarhouse they are an actual advantage—they let out more steam. All I still needed was some kind of top roofing to keep out rain. I could have used cedar shingles for $60.00, or cedar seconds like Thoreau for $40.00, or metal roofing for $25.00, or common asphalt shingles for $20.00. What I actually did use was asphalt paper, Bird's best quality with mineral surface, two rolls at $4.50 a roll. I used only half the second roll, giving the rest to a friend, a widow on Thetford Hill whose wood-shed had developed a leak. She later gave me an old but good foot-treadle grindstone that had belonged to her husband, so I think it is fair to deduct $2.25.

Furthermore, Thoreau had a string of expenses, all escaped by me, for hardware and fittings. We both made our own doors, and are even there. But he had to pay $2.43 for two secondhand windows, while I just walked out to the barn and picked my four out of a pile. Almost any old barn has enough windows lying around to equip two or three small houses. He had to spend fourteen cents for hinges and screws, and ten cents for a door latch. I got all the hinges and screws I needed from that heap of boards in the barn, and as for a door latch, I don't have one. An old iron ring serves to open the door, and I lock it with the padlock that used to be on the footlocker my wife took to college. Finally, he spent fifteen cents on

a mantle-tree iron and one cent for carpenter's chalk, bringing his total for one complete plaster-walled Cape Cod house with brick chimney and stone-based fireplace up to $28.12½. Per square foot of floor space, he had spent 18.8 cents. I don't need a mantle-tree iron, and I marked my sawcuts with a pencil I already owned. My total for one complete sugarhouse with two double windows and a white pine steam vent was $69.65. As I have eighty-eight square feet of floor space, the cost per square foot came to 79.1 cents.

Or, rather, it came to that for about three months, and then, the day after Thanksgiving, I betrayed everything *Walden* stands for. I had a six-inch slab of cement poured on top of the dirt floor. I had good reason. The worst thing that can happen when you're sugaring is to have your evaporator suddenly tilt to one side as its heat thaws the frozen ground. If this happens, your sap pans run dry on one side and instantly scorch. I heard enough stories during the summer about people with dirt-floored sugarhouses having to spend a year's profits on new pans that I finally got scared and ordered the cement. I am not sorry. And yet cement is modern. Cement comes from the world of aluminum siding and pink plumbing and giant revolving trucks. Even though a neighbor in the contracting business had my order added to a mixerload he was getting anyway, so that I had no delivery charge or any expense but the bare basic cost of one cubic yard of cement, the slab still jumped the cost of my house by 30 percent. I paid $21.38 for it, and my house has finally cost $91.03. That's more than Emerson paid for his whole eleven acres, and raises my cost to $1.03 per square foot of floor space.

But it turns out that even cement does not betray the point of *Walden*. The point is not to use quaint building methods; Thoreau himself consciously rejected the quaintness of 1845, which would, he says, have been to build a log cabin or a bark tepee, and used the latest thing, machine-made boards. The point is to simplify as much as possible, and so test the standard claims of one's time about the cost of things—an education, a house, a life. "I thus found that the student who wishes for a shelter can obtain one for a lifetime at an expense not greater than the rent which he now pays annually," Thoreau wrote in 1845. It's still true, Henry. Harvard students pay $580 a year for their rooms now, and Dartmouth students, not twelve miles from my sugarhouse, pay from $369 to $639. Men are still trying to solve the problem of a livelihood by formulas more complicated than the problem itself.

The Evaporator

A SUGARHOUSE, even one with a cement floor, is an empty shell. You need an evaporator to go inside. And that's where the serious cash outlay begins. There were no evaporators in Thoreau's time— people were still mostly boiling in iron kettles, which they had anyway, because their parents had used them to make soap. But as soon as evaporators did begin to come in, after the Civil War, screams of pained farmers about the price were heard all over New England. There was a conference of central Vermont sugar makers in 1872, for example, to discuss new equipment and methods. A Mr. Bisbee of Washington County was there specially to talk about his recently purchased evaporator. He liked both its speed and the high quality of the syrup it made. "His only objection to it was, that it cost about $90, when he thought it ought not cost more than $30."

Mr. Bisbee would have been a lot more upset in 1969, when prices of small evaporators started at around $375. (They're up to $400 now.) I wasn't delighted at the news myself, and my first thought was to look for a secondhand one. I let this fact be known in the general store in Thetford Center. That was on September third—a date I remember, because on that day I finished the sugarhouse. On September fourth I had a call from a young farmer up on Gove Hill named Malcolm Jamieson. Mickey said he had a little evaporator just the right size for me. He would let me have not only it but a good storage tank and sixty buckets, all for $200. Wonderful!

When I went up on Sunday to look, though, Mickey's turned out to be a single-pan rig. I knew just enough to know I didn't want it. Sugaring with one pan may be all right if you're a native, but for transplanted suburbanites the degree of excitement involved would be unbearable.

That statement needs explaining. All modern evaporators start with a long metal frame called an arch. At one end is a grate in which you build a fire, and the rest amounts to a piece of horizontal chimney. The arch is lined, sides and bottom, with bricks. The top is open, and that's where your pans sit. You build a fire in the grate, and it roars down the arch right under the pans. Then it turns and roars up a big stovepipe at the far end. By ancient rule, that pipe is twice as high as the arch is long. If flames come out the top of it, your fire may be a trifle high.

Now if you have a one-pan evaporator, first of all it has to be very small, because the one pan goes the whole length of the arch. The ones I've seen are all two feet by four. Secondly, the pan has to be flat-bottomed, since it's your syrup-making pan as well as your boiling pan. Both these facts make production rather slow.

But the serious objection for an amateur is that every little while you're finishing off a separate small batch of syrup, at which moment the least touch of panic means disaster. With a one-pan rig you sugar like this: You put your pan up on the arch, run ten or fifteen gallons of sap into it, and light the fire. In about an hour, if you have dry wood and a clean pan, you have reduced those fifteen gallons of sap to two quarts of maple syrup. Less, actually, since the average ratio of sap to syrup is thirty-two to one. The whole surface of the pan is bubbling wildly. Then, at just the right moment, you wrench open the side tap and draw off most but not quite all of the syrup into a filter. Then you start over with fifteen more gallons of sap. Unless, of course, you drew off too much syrup. In that case, you start scraping. During the few seconds after most of the syrup has run out and before much new sap has run in, the searing heat can easily dry out a corner of the pan. The syrup instantly becomes burnt maple sugar; and, if you're unlucky, tin plate begins to melt off the pan. A beginner is not up to that kind of excitement.

What I needed was a two-pan rig, in which sugaring is a continuous process and an error in judgment means nothing worse than slightly darker syrup. Sap is constantly flowing into the first pan and through a float valve from the first to the second. Unless you run out of sap (or unless you have a dirt floor and the whole arch tilts), there is no danger of a pan running dry. But no one in Thetford, or even in South Strafford or Norwich, seemed to have a two-pan evaporator for sale. When it got to be late September, and I didn't even have any leads, I decided to advertise for one. There are many ways of doing this, but only one I know of that is free. This is to put an ad in the kind of newspaper that most state departments of agriculture publish. In Vermont it is a biweekly called the *Agriview,* and in New Hampshire a weekly called the *Market Bulletin.* Since Thetford is on the border between the two states, I put my ad in both.

Both of these publications are very small and very informal. The *Agriview* is one eight-inch by twelve-inch sheet, printed on both sides; the *Market Bulletin* one double sheet. Both give produce prices, news of pesticide controls and county fairs, and lists of things like licensed livestock dealers. Both devote most of their space, though, to farmers' advertising. Want to sell a bull, buy a tractor, find a hired man? There's your place—provided, of course, you live in Vermont or New Hampshire. (An out-of-stater can put in a want ad, but you have to be a resident to list things for sale. Either way, it's free.)

Anyone who thinks that country life is dull should take a look at a few of these ads. The average city dweller probably does no more than twenty different things a week (read meters, watch

TV, eat; sell leather goods, go to museums, sleep; build engine blocks, mow the lawn, drink). The average farmer does hundreds. This diversity shows up plainly in the ads. Among the want ads placed in New Hampshire in the slack (for farming) month of December 1970, for example, are these:

By a man in Rumney who definitely lives on a private dirt road and who may have some distrust of public property: "Old horse- or truck-drawn gravel road grader; can need some repair. Mention if owned by town."

By someone in Amherst who must be putting up a new house or barn, and who is ready to start as far away from the finished building as Thoreau did: "Cement block machine."

By an absent-minded woodsman in Derry: "Will the man from Portsmouth who called me about Cedar logs please call again as have lost name and address."

By a man in East Kingston who is plainly in the process of moving from "living in the country" to part-time farming: "To exchange bay Shetland pony stallion, black mane and tail, 45 inches, proven breeder, value $100, for Hereford bull calf, 2 months or older, and pay difference."

By the owner of a chain saw in Merrimack: "To clear lots in exchange for hardwood and small pay; or single trees in exchange for wood. Weekend work only."

By a farmer in Raymond who has plainly kept livestock so long that he thinks of machinery as having feelings, too: "Used hay bale conveyor, 18-24 feet long, in reasonable condition. Will be used inside for light work." Reassuring the seller that his conveyor will be treated gently and kept in the barn, I find charming.

By another man in Raymond: "Would like my 1½-year-old Hampshire ewe bred nearby."

By a Yankee handyman in Keene who must be planning a little mill of some sort, and who works to a wide tolerance: "Used leather belting; would like it to be five inches wide, but could use six or even four."

By a couple in Hanover who are strong on either pollution control or low fuel bills: "Old farm to rent in the Lebanon area. Prefer wood heat."

And finally, and rather touchingly, an out-of-state ad. By a man in Fitchburg, Massachusetts, who clearly wants to get away from that same railroad that used to annoy certain people in Concord. (It ran and still runs right by the end of Walden Pond.) A job: "On dairy farm, with no milking, or on a horse farm. Have no experience. Also will accept job in lumber mill."

As for things for sale, I know where a man could get three good woods horses for $250 each, or six 300-pound pigs for $50 each. I know where he could get a 1929 Model AA tractor with snowplow for $200 or an almost new bulldozer for $6,900. I know where he could get 40,000 used bricks for five cents each, or a ton of dimensional granite for $20, or a registered Dorset ram in exchange for hay. (About a ton and a half, at winter hay prices, would do it.)

My ad, in late September 1969, said simply I

wanted a two foot by six foot evaporator in good condition. That's the smallest size of double-pan rig, and the one that would best fit my sugarhouse —which I was already wishing was bigger. If I had it to do over, I would get an evaporator first, and then build the sugarhouse around it.

I got four responses, three from retired farmers who said right away that their rigs were much bigger than two-by-six, but they would give me a nice price. The fourth was from a lady who had inherited a cousin's farm in Royalton, knew there was a sugarhouse, but had never looked inside. I went over, chiefly for the drive up the White River, which is a pretty one. As I suspected, it was a massive old four-by-fourteen evaporator, which not only wouldn't have fitted either in my truck or my sugarhouse, but which would have required the sap from at least 500 buckets just to keep running, and 1,000 is better. You need to be a full-time farmer to tend that many buckets, or at least to have a couple of teen-age children. Until mine get a good deal bigger—they're currently nine and six—I doubt if I go over a hundred.

The school year, and my job, had begun a little before the trip to Royalton. For the next month I was too busy teaching to think much about hunting evaporators. I might have thought about it weekends, except that weekends I had to think about fences. Our two beef cattle had taken to getting out of their pasture and going cross-lots to visit Harry Paige's milk cow. Every time I patched a place, they would break out somewhere else. After the third break it became obvious that our existing fence—rusty barbwire circa 1900, tottery cedar posts circa 1940—needed to be replaced. It took all the weekends into late October to do this, since it involved driving two hundred fence posts, and stringing three sixteen-hundred-foot strands of wire. At that point, putting away a spare quarter-mile reel of barbwire in the barn, I realized in some horror that in another few weeks there would be snow on the ground, that I had no evaporator or prospect of one, and that if I didn't look out it would get to be sugaring time and there I would be with a sugarhouse, maple trees, even some buckets, and no way to make syrup. I decided on the spot to buy a new rig.

The next Saturday a student and I drove over to Rutland, to G. H. Grimm and Company, manu-facturers of sugaring equipment and hay tedders. (Tedding is turning new-mown hay over so it will dry on the under side.) Grimm's is what all factories ought to be like, and hardly any are. The building is three-story clapboard, neither old nor new. At one end is an office for the owner and his two sons, and over it is a plain wooden-floored showroom with three or four evaporators set up. The rest of the building is factory. There are about a dozen employees scattered around, mostly skilled tinsmiths. Almost everything they do makes sense to the eye. One man is stamping out curved sap bucket lids with a sap-bucket-lid stamping machine. It's not a full-time job, just something he does occasionally when the stock of lids gets low. (I asked him.) Another is shaping—I almost want to say creating—a flue-bottomed sap pan out of nothing but solder and sheets of English tin. A third is making a small and quite beautiful tin pitcher. This turns out to be a hydrometer holder. A hydrometer is what you use to test when your syrup is ready to draw off, if you are being scientific. (I used a more primitive method last year, but I like the tin pitchers so much that now I have bought one and its accompanying hydrometer, to try this year. It's rather cozy science. A Grimm hydrometer consists of the usual glass tube with a bulb at the lower end—it would be at home in any lab. But in the bulb for weight is a neat little pile of bird shot, and in the tube for calibration is a strip of paper trimly hand-marked with the Brix scale for specific gravity of sugar solutions. The instrument makes sense to the eye, in the way a steam engine does and a diesel locomotive does not.)

One of the sons was on duty in the front office —the Grimm family no longer owns the factory, and this was a young man named Robert Moore.

He was just finishing selling a truckload of syrup cans to a farmer in a red cap from upstate New York. When the farmer left, I told him I wanted to buy a two-by-six evaporator, and very shortly I found myself in the showroom, trying to decide between a raised-flue ("Lightning") model and a dropped-flue ("Grimm") model. Same price for both.

He explained that the Grimm is a trifle faster but the Lightning a trifle more foolproof. It was the work of a second to pick the Lightning. No trouble choosing between a wood-fired and an oil-fired model, either. There is not a single oil well on my farm. The sale seemed all but made. But then Mr. Moore began picking up parts and explaining how to set the evaporator up when I got it home: where the floats go, which washers go where on the pan connectors, what the regulator is, how to lay the bricks (supplied by owner), how to reverse the heater pipe. It became clear to me that I'd never get the damn thing set up right, and even if I did, I wasn't smart enough to operate even a Lightning. I began to think longingly about iron kettles.

Normally under such circumstances I would avoid making a decision at all, by saying I wanted to go home and think it over for a couple of days. This time I couldn't. Mr. Moore had already given me a price list, with verbal annotations. Two-by-six evaporators had gone up from $340 to $375 on October 1, 1969. There was a ten-day grace period, which had already expired. But it was still October. If I would buy mine and take it home that day, I could have the old price. On Monday I would pay $35 more. Agony. The student and I went out and walked twice around the block while he laughed at me for getting a headache from pure indecisiveness. Then we went back in the factory, and I wrote Mr. Moore a check for $340, less 2 percent for cash, plus 3 percent for the Vermont sales tax, which comes to $343.20. (Like a good Vermonter, he did this as two separate calculations, deducting the 2 percent before adding the 3 percent, which saved me twenty cents in sales tax.) Then the student and I drove back to Thetford and stacked all the parts in the sugarhouse. I had to take them all out again when the cement floor was poured in November.

It's true. I never would have got the thing set up by myself. Fortunately, one of the three selectmen of Thetford is a carpenter and builder named George Stowell, who has been a passionate sugar maker all his life. He is an even busier man than Ken Bragg. But a new evaporator is a strong lure to him, and one Sunday morning in December he came over and bricked up the arch for me. I had the bricks (free ones from the Hanover Inn), and he provided the mortar. It took a lot of both. Then working in perfect silence he put every float and valve and bronze washer where it ought to go, and once it was all in place it made sense to the eye. The bill came to $18.28, for labor and one sack of cement. A complete evaporator, installed and ready to fire up, thus cost me $361.48. It should be capable of producing just about a gallon of syrup an hour.

Before he left, Mr. Stowell took an appreciative
look at the new red paint on the metal frame, and
at the shining pans, and his own trim brickwork.
"Nice to start with a new one," he said. "I got
mine in the Depression. Money was scarce. You
could hear a dime drop anywhere in Vermont.
But I'd saved a little here and there. Thought I'd

better get a new one. When I got her set up, I was prouder'n if I'd had a— a— Cadillac." He went so far as to give the back pan a friendly slap, as if it had been a horse's neck. "She'll last as long as you do."

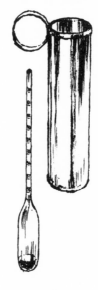

Hydrometer

Casks and Buckets

A SUGARHOUSE and an evaporator are all very well, but you still need sap. You have to get it out of the trees; you have to move it, usually several hundred yards, to the place where you're going to boil; and you have to store it when you get it there. All that means more equipment.

The easiest way to get sap out of a maple in the spring is to break off a twig. Sap will drip out of the broken end so fast as to be alarming, as if the tree had hemophilia. But it doesn't, and within a few hours the flow will stop. No one will ever run a sugar operation with a forest of weeping maples. For reliable supply, you've got to get access to the trunk.

The easiest way to do *that* is to hit the tree with an axe. And this is, in fact, what the early settlers did. Come spring, each farmer, grasping his narrow axe like Thoreau, would head for his sugar orchard. When he reached the first tree, he'd give it a good whack. If he were a careful man, he might give it three or four, grouped together in what the settlers called a "box." Then he'd swing his axe once more and give a final, slightly harder whack an inch below. Into this bottom cut he stuck a broad chip of wood. Sap would then trickle down the bark, out to the end of the chip, and drip into a little trough set underneath. The settler had made the trough himself, by the simple process of hollowing out a piece of pine log.

Gathering was equally simple. When a trough

got full, he lugged it to the nearest iron kettle, and dumped. He didn't have to walk any three hundred yards, either. A kettle can only handle the sap from a couple of dozen maples, because the boiling is so slow, so he had one set up in each clump of trees, suspended between two log posts. He built the first fire as soon as he dumped the first gallon of sap. Boiling then went on continuously for the rest of the season, nights and stormy days included. Total equipment required: one axe, forty or fifty homemade troughs, and a couple of kettles. Cash outlay: none.

The great flaw to the system was that it usually killed the trees within five years. Maples don't like being whacked. Not that the settlers cared; the woods were full of trees. When one patch of maples died, they just moved to another, taking their kettles with them. The love affair between Vermonters and maples had not yet begun. That affair began with the next generation, which found a gentler way of gathering sap. Tapping as now practiced began about 1800.

If he didn't already own one, the settler's son now bought an auger. Come spring, he put on his snowshoes and went out to that part of the sugar orchard that had survived his father. When he reached the first tree, he took the auger and drilled a small hole in the trunk, two inches deep and two or three feet up from the ground. (The lower you tap a maple, the faster the sap flows.) Into this hole he put a neat little wooden spout, which he had made by splitting a piece of elderberry branch and taking out the pith. On the snow underneath he set a good cedar bucket, which he had gone out and bought for cash. Maples probably don't enjoy being drilled, either, but it doesn't hurt them. They can survive it for a hundred years and still be producing good sap.

As for gathering, the son now did it with a team of horses, a sled, and a wooden gathering tank, also bought for cash. He himself sat comfortably on the sled and drove slowly through the orchard, while his children ran from tree to tree, emptying the buckets. This is the system still to be found in the pictures that ornament fancy syrup cans—and it has by no means vanished in real life, either. I know a man over near Corinth who farms with a tractor eleven months a year. But along in March he hitches two horses to a sled and sets off to sugar. I used to think it was pure sentiment, until I teased him about it once. "You ever see a tractor stop when you shout 'Whoa!' " he asked me. I never have. I should explain that his children are grown and gone—he empties his own buckets now. With a tractor he'd have to stop at each tree, get down, dump the buckets, climb back up, and drive to the next tree. With the team he can just walk along, while they follow at his call. You don't have to put a horse into neutral.

Going back to 1800, when the settler's son had a full tank, he drove his sled down to the boiling place. That might still be a collection of iron kettles standing out in the open. More likely he had a sugarhouse, with the kettles inside, and a dry place to store wood. It is even possible that he might have a homemade flat pan. Either way, he probably owned a huge wooden storage tank, into which he now drained his little wooden gathering tank. (Sugar tanks were rated, and still are, in units of a barrel, a barrel being thirty-one gallons. The smallest gathering tank is a three-barrel; storage tanks now go up to fifty barrels.) He had a lot more expensive equipment than his father, but he also made five or ten times as much sugar.

Later generations introduced a great many refinements, all adding to the cost. The first was that pre-Civil War luxury item, nails. A bucket sitting on snowy ground will quite readily tip over when it's full. To avoid this, farmers began to drive a nail in below each elderberry spout, and hang the bucket on the tree. They stopped again long ago, but the habit still affects New England behavior. Sawmills even now hate to cut up the butt log of an old maple, unless it comes from deep woods. Strike one old sugaring nail, buried deep in the tree, and you spend the next hour filing saw teeth.

From the modest start with nails, metal gradually took over everything. First the wooden spouts went, being replaced by patent metal ones from which you can hang the buckets directly. Wooden buckets were the next to go, about ninety years ago. (The Vermont Board of Agriculture did a survey in 1882, and found farmers divided fifty-fifty between cedar and the new tin variety.) Then metal lids appeared—buckets had previously been open to the weather. By 1900, the great wooden tanks were giving way to light metal ones. Tin buckets themselves faded before the rush of galvanized. Except on syrup cans, tractors and pickup trucks mostly took over from horses and sleds.

But the bucket-and-tank system itself remains in vigorous use. A man who went into small-scale sugaring today would probably adopt it; and a man who had sugared in 1870 or even in 1800 would recognize and understand every piece of equipment. He might whistle a little at the prices, low as these are compared to most industrial prices now. A man in the 1970s getting all new equipment, and taking full advantage of quantity discounts, would buy the following:

100 sixteen-quart galvanized buckets	$120.00
100 lids	35.00
100 spouts	15.00
1 three-barrel gathering tank	80.00
1 eight-barrel storage tank .	62.00
1 7/16" tapping bit	2.25
1 spout driver	1.25
10' of 2½" rubber hose	21.00
	———
	$336.50

That would set him up, though there's plenty more he could buy if he wanted to. If he were both rich and lazy, he might, for example, get a Sap Pump Sucker to mount behind his gathering tank. This is a powerful gasoline engine with a fifty-foot hose attached. You take the end of the hose in your hand and walk from tree to tree, sticking it in each bucket, the contents of which then vanish with a thwoop. A Sap Pump Sucker is said to drain a sixteen-quart bucket in twelve seconds. Very convenient, if you don't have horses. It will, however, cost you $183.

He could also get a gasoline-powered drill for tapping. In fact, anyone who hangs more than five hundred buckets would be well advised to. Only effete types, I feel, would for a hundred. It would cost him another $103.

And if his orchard were on a hillside—Vermont *is* mostly hillside—and his sugarhouse were down at the bottom, he could install a pipeline, just like a Texas oilman. He would run a two-inch main straight up the hill, and lay out smaller spur lines on both sides. Every fifty feet or so he would install a dumping station, which is simply a large funnel tapped into the pipe. Then he could watch gravity take the sap down to his sugarhouse, absolutely free. Gravity and wood are the chief natural resources of a Vermont farm.

I almost built such a pipeline last year. My trees are in two locations: a row along the road, which I can easily tend by truck, and a grove on the lower slopes of Tucker Hill. A 650-foot pipeline (I was going to cheat and make it one-inch, which meant I could have installed it for about $70) would have put sap right in the sugarhouse. The trouble is that the pipe would have had to cross the pasture, which usually has two cows and two horses in it. If I simply laid the pipe on the ground, the horses would step on it and trip over it and probably break it. If I buried it, then the sap would always collect and freeze in the two places where the pasture has a little dip. Unless I went below frost line, and *that* would mean hiring a backhoe to dig a trench four feet deep. In the end carrying buckets to the road is easier.

If I had put in a pipeline, it would have been plastic pipe. This is highly symbolic. Some day plastic may drive metal out of sugaring, just as metal once drove wood. In fact, one new method has come in since World War II that does away with metal and with buckets at one stroke. You just buy a lot of thin plastic tubing—it costs four cents a foot—and after you drill your holes, you rig up the trees for intravenous bleeding. You can let the sap come at its own pace, or—this is the latest wrinkle—you can install a vacuum pump down at the sugarhouse and suck it out whether the tree is in the mood or not. You are said to get about fifty percent more from each taphole that way. Some people also think it's as hard on the maples as whacking them with an axe, but the system is too new for anyone to be sure yet.

I, of course, have buckets. For an operation as small as mine, it wouldn't be worth the trouble of setting up all that plastic tubing, and I freely admit to aesthetic motives as well. Long ago sap buckets assumed a classical form. They are the aristocrats of the bucket world: tall and slender, with a nice taper from top to bottom. This is for the highly practical reason that it makes them easy to stack, but there is no denying the elegance. Furthermore, a big maple with three or four buckets strung round it has a kind of flag-and-bunting festival look which gives me fresh pleasure every spring. Whereas a sugar orchard put to plastic tubing just looks like the intensive-care unit of some outdoor hospital.

At the time I built the sugarhouse, I had already

lived first in New Hampshire for two years and then in Vermont for nine, and I had been making a driblet of maple syrup right along. I obviously already had some equipment. Specifically, I had forty-one buckets, five lids, and five spouts. The five spouts were my first sugaring equipment. I

found them in an old shed on the place I rented when I first came up here. Finding them was what decided me to start sugaring in the first place, only I needed buckets to go with them. At that time I didn't know where to buy equipment; in fact, I had only just learned to recognize sugar maples. (Don't forget they have no leaves in

March, which makes it harder. There are many legends of outsiders earnestly tapping red maples or even elms, while the natives grin behind their hands.)

But my wife had a couple of plastic scrub buckets, the kind you get in a hardware store for eighty-nine cents, or did ten years ago. There being no natural color for plastic, these were mandatorily cheerful, and came in a choice of bright yellow, blue, or pink. Hers were pink. I bought three more, yellow ones, and tapped two big maples in the front yard. The sight of maples with pink and yellow buckets so amused some of my neighbors that they didn't even bother to conceal their grins. One of them asked me if I didn't want to get Snow White and the seven dwarfs to help me gather. All the same, I made three quarts of maple syrup in the kitchen that year, not even hurting the wall paper. (I didn't know about the risk, anyway.)

Plastic scrub buckets have a great drawback, though, in lacking lids. Rain and snow come in freely. I can support the complaint of an old farmer named W. O. Brigham who asked bitterly in 1878, "How often do we boil twelve to twenty-four hours to evaporate the water caught in a single storm?" Furthermore, whatever kind of plastic those buckets were made of was not designed for freezing New England nights. Before the season was over, both pinks and one of my new yellows had splits in the bottom. Part of my hatred of plastic dates from that spring.

By the next year I had learned my way around a bit more. When sugaring time came, I had proper sap buckets on hand—far more than can be used in a kitchen operation—and I had lids. The buckets I got at an auction in the hamlet of Sawnee Bean, Vermont (apparently named for a medieval Scottish cannibal, no one knows why). A man named Messer was selling everything on his farm, including several hundred good galvanized sap buckets. They went in stacks of whatever size the auctioneer happened to pick up. I bid on a lot of forty-one, and got them at twenty-two cents each. Since I refuse to count the plastic pails, and since the five spouts were free, my first equipment cost was $9.02 for these buckets. I had expected to get some of Messer's lids, too, but whether because it started snowing or he simply got bored, the auctioneer put up the four or five hundred lids as one lot, which I was not quick-witted enough to bid on. (I could have resold most of them, probably at a nice profit, to all the other people who had bought thirty or forty buckets.) So I made five extremely clumsy lids myself out of a piece of old tin roofing; and as long as I was boiling in the kitchen, these were all I needed and more. The sap from about three buckets is what you can conveniently evaporate over a gas burner on a stove. Until last year, my expenses remained $9.02.

With a sugarhouse and an evaporator, though, I needed more of everything, and I didn't plan to buy it new. Instead I studied the *Agriview*. In January 1970, a farmer named Wallace Illsley up in Randolph put in an ad saying he had a couple of hundred buckets and a gathering tank for sale. When I phoned him about the tank, he said guardedly that I might not want it, it was pretty old, and I said I might's well come look. The drive to Randolph is a pretty one, too.

Mr. Illsley and a vet were doing the annual checkup on his milk cows when I got there on a zero morning. I waited, in the company of all the barn cats, in a place where a corner caught the sun and probably brought the temperature up to twenty. When the vet left, Mr. Illsley and I drove up the road a quarter of a mile to an old barn he uses for storage, and climbed up to the loft. At first all I could see in the semidarkness was a huge pile of boards about like the ones in my barn cellar. A little less rotten, maybe. Then Mr. Illsley got the hay door open, and a flood of sun came in. There, surrounded by stacks of rusty tin buckets, was the tank.

It was not just beautiful but stunning. It was white pine, bound with iron straps, a perfect conic section. Four feet across at the bottom and three at the top. Flawless coopering of probably around 1890. Dirty, weathered grey with age, a little splintered, but sound. It did need a new hose. The two-inch rubber one that came out near the bottom was crumpled and patched, and obviously should have been replaced thirty years ago. Easy enough to do it now. As soon as I stuck my head in the pouring door in the top and failed to see any pinpoints of light—and so knew there were no leaks—I had to have it.

But I have learned a little in ten years. What I said was that I really had a metal tank in mind, but what about those old thirteen-quart buckets? What did he want for them? Pick 'em over, he said, and you can have any you want for ten cents each. Same with the lids. He added that he'd bought up the contents of an old ruined sugarhouse two farms away, kept what he wanted, and this up here was what was left.

The buckets were in fact in terrible shape, but eventually I found ten that seemed worth taking. The lids were even worse, not much better than my five homemade ones, besides being filthy. But I picked out ten of them, too, meanwhile coming on a wooden box full of spouts—a collection of just about all the types made between 1870 and 1930. We agreed I'd look them over back at the house, it being probably a little below zero in that barn. Mr. Illsley said I could take what I wanted for three cents each. "Guess you don't want the tank," he added casually.

"Well, I might get it," I said even more casually. "It *is* sound. What are you asking for it?"

"Sound? You won't find a tighter one," he said. "What would you want to pay for it?"

I observed that it needed a new hose, and he agreed. Then I said I wanted to pay what it was worth. He said, well, twenty-five dollars seemed about right, and after a suitable hesitation I agreed. It was the perfect kind of deal. Each of us was sure he had skinned the other, and in a sense each of us was right. One reason I think Mr. Illsley felt that way is that he proceeded to throw in an eleventh bucket and lid free.

Together we rolled that huge tank over to the hay door, and then pushed it out—something you couldn't do in Florida. Two feet of snow on the ground has certain advantages as a cushion. While I gathered up my buckets and lids, he picked up the box of spouts, and we started on down. Back at the house I sorted out fifty of the more recent ones. To match his generosity with the buckets, I also bought a quart of syrup, so pale and rich looking as to justify the old name of maple honey. Mrs. Illsley packed it for me in a spotlessly clean mayonnaise jar. I paid him $28.50 for the tank, eleven buckets and lids, and fifty spouts, and another $2.00 for the syrup, and started on home. I have since washed the tank, sanded it, put on a new hose, and painted it with two coats of the best (and, alas, most expensive) paint I know. The color is Haddam Barn Red, which is to ordinary barn red as fresh cream is to Coffee Mate. The four iron straps are black. Hose and paint together cost me $6.00. Now that the tank is smartly dressed, a couple of people have said it ought to be in a sugaring museum, but what I like to see is something doing the work it was made for. Mine, indeed, does double work, since I use it both for gathering and storage, and sugar directly from the back of the truck.

Later in the winter I picked up forty good lids from Mickey Jamieson for $5.00. At the same time I threw away four of my five homemade ones. So having now fifty-two buckets and lids, fifty-five spouts, and a good four-barrel tank, I was about ready to sugar. This first year's equipment had cost me $48.52. Add the house and the evaporator, and I had spent a grand total of $501.03.

All I still needed to do before spring was to get up a little more wood, to add to the pile I had made when clearing the site. For logs I simply took all the pieces in the woodshed that had refused to go through the door of our wood stove. We keep one going most of the winter in what Henry Stevens would call the front room, and we call the living room. And for kindling and fast wood, I cut up that old board pile in the barn cellar. One of the advantages of sugaring is that it en-ables you to get rid of all the old lumber around a farm that's too good to throw away and not good enough to use. Most of those boards were sawed out before the Civil War, and they've had time to get nice and dry. They burn hot. That done, the next move was up to the maple trees.

Steam Coming Out the Vent

FOR SOME REASON, town meeting day in Vermont
—the first Tuesday after the first Monday in
March—is almost always warm and sunny. Winter has by no means ended. It is going to snow
again at least three or four times. Fields won't be
starting to green up until mid-April. Lilacs and
apple blossoms won't be out until May. But when
you get home from town meeting at two or three

in the afternoon, the temperature is up to sixty. Snow water is dripping from all the eaves, and you can almost hear the maples pumping sap. It is irresistible to hang a few buckets. Even though you remember clearly from last year that the sap ran only one day, and then the temperature stayed below forty for a week and you didn't get another drop, the afternoon is just too nice to waste.

Town meeting day in 1970 was like the rest: blue skies and a cunning semblance of spring. A little after three P.M. my daughters and I emerged from the barn. I was carrying a brace and bit, a hammer, and a clean sap bucket containing a pile of freshly washed spouts. Lily, the nine-year-old, was staggering behind me with a stack of buckets; and Margaret, the six-year-old, came last with the lids. It was hard walking, because there was still two feet of snow on the ground, and the crust had completely rotted since morning.

We were heading for a row of hundred-year-old maples along the road in front of our house. They are fortunately on the higher side of the road, so that only a little highway salt gets to them. With luck, they won't be completely killed for another twenty years. (I have already started their replacements: a row of saplings dug up in the woods, set halfway between each of the old trees and ten feet further back from the road. They should be ready for tapping soon after the year 2000. I hope to be sitting on the front porch, quavering advice.)

When our procession reached the first tree, I went around to the south side, where sap usually runs best, and found a place directly under a big branch where there was no scar from an old tap. I drilled the first hole, and hammered in a spout. A few seconds later sap began dripping out, the drops in such quick succession that it was almost a tiny stream. A fraction of a second after that, all the buckets and all the lids were in the snow, and the girls were fighting over who would be the first to put her mouth up to the spout and get the year's first drink of new sap. I have often

wondered if the settlers, with eight or ten children each, and their troughs just sitting on the
ground, didn't lose a lot of sap. Parental discipline
must have been sterner then.

By four o'clock we had eighteen buckets up,
two on the southerly side of each front tree. Even
from the house you could hear one of the nicest
of all spring sounds, which is the ping of sap dripping into empty buckets. You don't get that with

plastic tubing. I don't suppose you got it with the old wooden buckets, either.

The rest of my buckets I planned not to hang until mid-March. I didn't have them all washed, anyway. But if there was a good early run, I'd at least get some of it. And there was. Thursday and Friday were both warm after freezing nights, and by Saturday most of the buckets were full, and the rest at least half. These were sixteen-quart buckets from Messer, which means that I had sixty-some gallons of sap to play with. By kitchen standards, this is a formidable quantity.

Saturday was another blue and gold day, and the minute I stepped outside, I knew I was not only going to gather but to try my first boiling. I had had Mr. Illsley's tank soaking since Tuesday, and it was now fully taken up and ready to use. Also remarkably heavy. By tipping it up on one side and then using my thighs as a fulcrum, I was just able to hoost it into the back of the truck.

Even with the girls to help, it took longer than I had expected to empty eighteen buckets. A truck, of course, won't come when called, and I was constantly in and out of the cab driving it another few feet down the road. Furthermore, a full sap bucket is impossible for a small girl to carry, and not easy even for a grown man. It has no handle, it weighs about thirty pounds, and it sloshes terribly. (That's why I've since been back to Grimm's and bought two flare-lipped gathering pails for $9 each.) We probably spilled six or eight gallons in the process of gathering.

To my dismay, the tank had only about a foot of sap in the bottom when we were done, and the thought did cross my mind that it would be prudent to wait a few days before boiling. I could use today to wash the rest of the buckets, and maybe paint the Illsley ones. I firmly repressed the thought, though, and we drove on down the hundred feet from the last tree to the sugarhouse. The sun was high, and the rapid ping of sap dripping into the newly empty buckets sounded reassuring. There'd be a few more gallons by noon, if I needed them.

I had worked out my plans long before. Not having a storage tank, I intended to run sap into the evaporator directly from the truck. The dirt road where it goes past the sugarhouse is about eighteen inches higher than the house site. (If you'd asked me that morning, I would have said three feet.) With the added elevation of the truck, I could easily park at the edge of the road and pipe in by gravity. An hour's boiling, and I'd have a gallon of syrup—the pale delicate fancy grade that you get from the very first sap. Other years I thought I'd done well to get three or four baby-food jars of first-run.

In actual fact, it took more than an hour just to get the sap flowing. I had long ago bought twenty feet of one-inch plastic pipe ($3.60 at Nichols Hardware in Lyme, New Hampshire) and attached one end to the intake valve of the evaporator. It took about a minute to fit the other end into a coupling and the coupling into the new hose on my tank. When nothing at all happened, my first thought was to unhook the evaporator end and try sucking on it, as people do when siphoning gas. Again nothing happened. It was Lily who found the ice plug where the pipe sagged lowest in the middle, and she and Mag who worked an eight-inch lump of ice out with their hands. The next suck got me a mouthful of sap (it beats gasoline), but no stream followed. Not enough elevation. Eventually I worked a couple of old beams under the tank, raising it another six inches. Then at last the evaporator began to fill with a steady gurgling sound. While it filled, the girls and I laid a fire in the grate, chiefly of alder branches and barn boards. Then I opened the steam vents and lit the fire.

You get a superb draft with an evaporator, and about two minutes later the first wisp of steam arose from the sap. A minute or two after that, the red paint began to blacken on the furnace doors, and at the same instant the first little wave of boiling began. Shortly thereafter the whole back pan went into a rolling boil, and a continuous eight-square-foot cloud of white steam began ascending to the steam vent and out both sides of it. I rushed out the door to see what it looked like from outside. What it looked like is hard to describe. For some reason the sugarhouse reminded me of a Viking helmet, the great plumes of steam, now gold-colored in the sunlight, being the horns. This mass of steam coming out in perfect silence and then floating away on the wind also reminded me by an even looser association of a clipper ship leaving port with sails just up. But all it actually looked like, I suppose, is a sugarhouse in the spring.

Shrieks from Lily brought me back in. Both pans were now boiling at high speed, and a thick, yellowy-white foam had formed all over the surface and was beginning to mount rapidly in the corners. I was prepared for it. Included with the evaporator had come a tin skimmer—an instrument like a trim, very narrow dustpan, with perforations all over the bottom. For the first time I skimmed the pans. Some sugar makers fling the foam on the floor, but I was (and am) too proud of my new sugarhouse, and sent it flying out into the snow. The sap had already taken on a faint tinge of color, and enough was going out as steam so that the float valves had opened, and a steady stream was flowing in from the truck to the first pan and from the first pan to the second.

a Skimmer

Just after I finished skimming and putting a little more wood on the fire, I learned a new social fact about Vermont. I see no truth at all to the myth that New Englanders are taciturn—they love gossip as well as anyone I ever knew—but the talk takes place mostly on neutral ground: in stores and barnyards, at auctions and church suppers. Your house is private. Vermonters are less likely to drop in unannounced for coffee than most other Americans, or to have you over for the evening. There are about two hundred people in Thetford Center, and I would guess I know a hundred and ninety of them. But I have not been in more than a dozen houses, and most people have never been in mine.

A different custom prevails for sugarhouses. Steam had been rolling out for about fifteen minutes now, and people in the village had had time to see it. I don't say they came pouring out of their houses and down to visit, but one or two at a time, a remarkable number did appear. First came Gordon Fifield, who lives just across the covered bridge, with stories about sugaring when he was a boy. Then Rob Hunter. Then a man, actually not from the village at all, who delivers milk for Billings Dairy. (He's not the same milkman I bought two pigs from a few years ago, but his successor.) Then Russell Jamieson—Mickey's father—who happened to be passing in his truck. I am clear that if I ever build another sugarhouse that's visible from a traveled road, I will make it considerably larger than eight feet by eleven. Ken Bragg's, which I was in for the first time just recently, is probably about right. There's room in his, on one side of the evaporator, and not crowding it any, for a row of armchairs.

It was Russell who pointed out to me that I was just about to have an emergency. I was so busy talking and skimming and keeping Margaret from opening the draw-off tap that I hadn't noticed that the stream of new sap had ceased coming in. The level in the back pan was sinking fast. Most sugar makers keep a bucket of water standing by for such cases, and I had one, too. But you hate to thin your sap that way; and while Russell opened the grate doors to chill the fire, I rushed out to check the tank. There was about three inches of sap left in the bottom, but not a drop flowing. I tipped it up on its side and held it long enough to run most of the remaining sap in, and then I let my fire go out and closed down for the day, without having made any syrup at all. What I had in the back pan was about twenty gallons of a pale amber fluid, perceptibly thicker and sweeter than sap, but nothing like syrup. In the little flat-bottomed front pan I had a couple of gallons of some stuff sweet enough so that Maggie and Lily each drank a cupful with relish (you set the cup on a snowbank for a couple of minutes first to cool it), but probably no more than half-way to syrup. I had been boiling for just over an hour. That afternoon it snowed a little, the temperature dropped, and the sap quit running.

I hung the rest of my buckets the next Saturday. That is, I hung another twenty-two, since I never had got the Illsley buckets painted, and one Messer bucket was down in the sugarhouse full of water. It was good sugar weather, and the sap was running briskly. Four days after that I had a day off from school and spent it boiling again. Willis Wood, the student who had come with me to buy the evaporator, worked with me. This time the gathering tank was full to the top when we started, which meant we had 125 gallons.

The partly boiled sap in the pans had been sitting there eleven days, but it was frozen solid. I don't believe it had deteriorated much—any more than frozen orange juice does in a grocer's counter. It was not only thawed but steaming within six or seven minutes of the time we started the fire. It soon did more. I had been content the previous time to keep the surface of the pans at a brisk rolling boil. But Willis is more adventuresome. He said his Cousin Augustus down in Weathersfield, who is eighty-two and who has sugared every spring for seventy years now, kept the sap in *his* pans leaping up like storm waves breaking on a rocky coast. Otherwise you're just fooling around, said Willis.

With my reluctant consent, he began stuffing barn boards into the fire as fast as they'd go. A sort of low murmur went over the pans, the column of steam visibly thickened, and for the first time a cloud bank began to build up under the sugarhouse roof. All the windows misted over simultaneously. Then the whole surface of boiling sap surged up, something like fifty pots on a stove all boiling over at once. (This is no exaggeration, but a slight understatement. I checked. My wife's pots range from saucepans five inches in diameter to one big ten-incher for cooking corn on the cob. Her two favorites are sixes. When one of them boils over, a twenty-eight-square-inch surface surges up. With the evaporator, 1,728 square inches of boiling surface are involved, or sixty-one pots' worth.) Just before there was a flood, Willis slammed the draft shut, and the whole surface gradually sank down again, still boiling hard. He opened it part way, and it started back up. We seemed doomed to fool around.

At that point something Russell Jamieson told me popped into mind. I had known all along that syrup pans sometimes surge up, though I hadn't realized it was quite so dramatic. I knew from Grimm's catalogue that there was a chemical on the market called Atmos 300, which is supposed to prevent this. But I had no idea of putting Atmos

300 in my sap, any more than I would plant stilbestrol pellets under the skin behind a calf's ear to force him to grow faster. That's not farming, that's outdoor chemistry.

I also had heard of a nineteenth-century technique for keeping pans from boiling over, which is to suspend a little piece of pork fat from a rafter, so that it dangles over your back pan, just below the rim. When the boiling sap leaps up and touches it, just enough gets melted to stop the high boiling. It can't really make maple sugar taste like pork fat, or Vermont sugar wouldn't have kept its good reputation. But I wasn't attracted to the pork-fat system, either.

Russell, though, was a dairy farmer for thirty years, and he knows a lot of dairy tricks. He had described the magical effect when you let one drop of cream fall onto the stormy surface of an evaporator. While Willis stayed to tinker with the draft and keep skimming, I hurried up to the house. We turned out not to have any cream, but we did have a pint of Billings Coffee-Cereal Special. When I came back with it, we opened the draft full, waited until the upward surge began, and then I stuck my finger in the Coffee-Cereal Special, and let one drop fall into the pan. It does look like magic. The whole pan quits tossing at once, and even the humming sound dies away, though the column of steam rises as thickly as before. I always keep a little jar of cream on a handy snowbank now.

This being a weekday morning, there were fewer visitors than there had been the first time. But one of the town listers—in most of America they're called tax assessors—did show up in mid-morning. He said he wanted to ask me some questions about a piece of land I had sold. I think he also wanted to watch a little sugaring, and reminisce. It was no moment to sit down and chat, because with our new fast-boil system we were getting to have something very close to maple syrup in the front pan. Willis and I were just hesitating whether to draw the first batch off. In other years, making a half-pint at a time on the kitchen stove, I had judged the product by taking a little out in a teaspoon and seeing if it tasted right. It always tasted delicious, and the syrup fairly often turned out later to be a little thin. No harm when it's for home consumption, but now I was a commercial producer. All the same, we had some in the scoop now, and were tasting.

The lister watched for a moment, and then asked us if we knew about aproning. Neither of

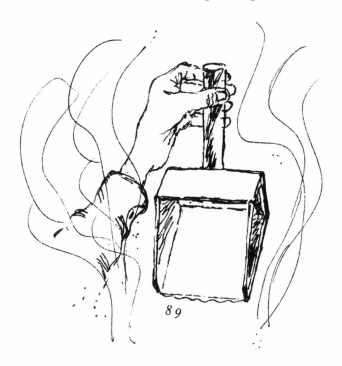

us did. (Cousin Augustus has an ancient hydrom-eter.) So he took the scoop, dipped it in the finishing pan, and then held it vertically over the pan until the last drops were trembling on the edge. Then they aproned. Instead of falling, they slowly merged until there was a little curving apron across the rim of the scoop, looking rather like maple taffy. "Draw her off, boys," he said triumphantly, and we did. We got a gallon and a half of fine first-run syrup.

Mr. Bisbee back in 1872 would have left the syrup standing a couple of days to let the nitrates and the sugar sand settle out, and then canned it cold. (Or, more likely, he would have taken it on down to maple sugar, which formed 90 percent of the crop in those days.) Willis and I ran ours through a double filter: an inner paper one and an outer felt one, both of which I had bought at Grimm's. $3.25 for the felt, 35 cents for the paper. The felt will last indefinitely; some people throw away a paper one after using—and washing—it no more than eight or ten times. Then we canned the first gallon on the spot, put a quart in a jar for Willis to take home as pay, and left the last quart still slowly dripping through. Before lunch we made another gallon.

I had a good supply of cans ready, having saved them up for five years from all the syrup we had bought, which was a couple of gallons a year. The one to three quarts I had been making myself each spring never even lasted until summer. I have a feeling you're not supposed to reuse Vermont Sugarmakers Association cans, but I have been careful never to ask. Anyway, I am not alone in reusing them. There used to be a hardware store in White River Junction—a tall old store full of parts for plough harness and big wooden hayrakes—that always had a whole tableful of them for sale, rather like the bookstores on Fourth Avenue in New York that sell slightly used review copies of new books at half price.

When the season ended on April sixteenth, I had made eight and a half gallons from forty buckets. A little low, but then I got half the buckets up late. Three gallons I kept for my family, and one I gave away. Willis Wood got a quart for pay, and so did Gary Fifield, a Thetford Academy senior who is roughly Gordon's second cousin. He dropped in at the third boiling, and stayed to work. That left four gallons to sell, all of which I sold in half-gallon cans at $4 each, for total cash receipts of $32. In each case the buyer was someone I knew who was aware he was getting his syrup in a secondhand though spotless can. I didn't grade it, because I didn't have a state grading set. In my opinion, what I sold was all Grade A. The Fancy grade I either kept or gave as presents; and the one gallon that was clearly Grade B I also kept, because Lily loves it strong and dark.

As against total expenditures of $508.23—I have now added in the plastic pipe and the filters —$32.00 is a fairly poor return. It would be even worse if I figured in any value for the several hundred hours of my time I put in building the house and sugaring, or counted truck time to Royalton, Randolph, and Rutland. Furthermore, most of the profit I immediately spent on the two gathering pails and the hydrometer. But I have three lines of defense against critical comment.

First, this was my prentice year. I expect to do better in the future. This year I expect to hang sixty buckets (an evaporator the size of mine will handle up to two hundred) and to get a full quart from each. That will be fifteen gallons, of which I expect to sell ten or eleven. Even granting that this time I'll be paying for new half-gallon cans at 38½ cents each, net receipts will be in the neighborhood of $75. In time, as Lily and Margaret get stronger and we hang more buckets, they may reach $100 and even more.

Second, there is the question of what I would be doing if I weren't sugaring. I observe that many of my fellow teachers put in *their* spare time in March getting in a little late skiing, going to the movies, and watching hockey on television. Their receipts are invariably $0.00, and what with lift tickets and Head skis and one thing and another, their expenses often exceed mine. Nor do they wind up with a year's supply of syrup. On the contrary, most of them feel they can't afford decent syrup for their own pancakes, and are getting supermarket stuff which is 6 percent maple or $5\frac{1}{2}$ percent maple or—this is superstition, not flavor—2 percent maple. The ones who mostly watch movies, as a matter of fact, don't even dare eat pancakes, because they are afraid of getting fat. Whereas if they were getting out the frock and milking stool, or hanging a few buckets, they could eat what they pleased.

But my last line of defense is the one I put most stock in. Sugaring, even on a much larger scale than mine, is not really a commercial operation. It is that happiest of combinations, a commercial affair which is also an annual rite, even an act of love. I will quote two old sugar makers as evidence. One is a man named L. C. Davis of South Reading, Vermont. In 1878 he gave a speech to an audience he addressed as "Brother Farmers." He began by quoting Thomas Jefferson on farming in general ("Tillers of the soil are the chosen of the Lord"), and then he launched into sugaring techniques—about as much from the point of view of the maple tree as that of the farmer. Mr. Davis felt, for example, that no maple, even the biggest, should be asked to handle more than one spout. But he had noticed many of his neighbors putting in three or even four, just as I do. (I go by a rule which says don't tap a tree until it's ten inches in diameter. One spout from there to eighteen inches, then two, and so on up to a maximum of four.) Mr. Davis could not have approved less. "To such I would say: you ought to have a guardian put over you, and if the trees could speak, they would have it done. Why will you abuse this most noble of trees, the sugar maple?" These are not the words of a businessman—though Mr. Davis made good money out of sugaring—but of a lover.

My other witness, Lyman Newton of Fairfield, was not so much in love with maple trees as he was with Vermont itself. But he expressed his love through the spring rites at the evaporator. In

1885 he gave a speech before the State Board of Agriculture. He started by talking about sugar in general, dwelling on its plebian origin. (Beets! Sorgo grass!) Then he turned to sugar in its lordly condition. His style rises—slightly—to the occasion. Echoes of the King James Bible can be heard in his normally flat storekeeper prose.

"Here in Northern Vermont we neither raise the Southern cane nor the Western sorghum, neither do we make beet sugar; but we are credited with making a superior article of maple sugar, a kind of sweet that when made with care retains its moisture and rich aromatic flavor, rendering it more acceptable to consumers than the most refined and highly-scented candies of the confectioner; and where introduced is almost always sure to sell, and especially is this the case among those who spent their childhood and youth in a maple sugar country. Hence the West has become to us a market for maple sugar. Vermonters have gone everywhere, and when spring comes they remember, like the children of Israel, not the leeks and garlics but the sugar works of their native hills. . . . And they attempt, although many times vainly, to satisfy their appetite by going to the grocery, where they inquire of the proprietor if he has Vermont maple sugar on hand, and they are informed that 'he has a small lot of *new* direct from the East,' and without waiting to investigate, they make a purchase. They get about as near Vermont maple sugar as oleomargarine is like Vermont butter."

When you're producing a sacred article, you don't have to maximize your cash return.

Postscript

SINCE I WROTE the last chapter, the 1971 season has come and gone. It was a deceitful one, even beyond the average. All through February there were signs of a forward spring. The chickadees began to mate early. (You don't have to be a voyeur to notice when they start, because they quit trilling "chickadee-dee-dee" and start loudly calling *"PHEE-BE."* For years I thought it *was* phoebes.) The snow fleas appeared at least a week ahead of time. In late February we had a thunderstorm—according to local lore, a guarantee of coming spring. And, sure enough, March first and second were unusually warm and sunny. I held out for twenty-four hours. But on March second, along with a good many other people, I went on and hung some buckets.

That's what the weather was waiting for. It turned cold that night. On March fourth, six inches of snow fell. On March eighth school was canceled in Thetford because of a small blizzard: another fifteen inches had come sliding down, and the wind turned it into drifts. On March tenth it was four below zero when Lily and Margaret left for school.

During all that time no sap ran, or almost none. It began to again on March twelfth, and that day I hung another thirty buckets. A friend named Kendrick Putnam, who lives just over the river in Lyme, New Hampshire, was sugaring with me. He has trees and buckets, but no evaporator. Too wary to tap out on the second (Ken has lived around here all his life and is consequently less optimistic about the weather than I), he, too, put up buckets on the twelfth. No blizzard followed, but no sugar weather, either. On a nice afternoon it might get up to thirty-eight, and a little sap would run languidly from trees on southern slopes. Most buckets, when you went to empty them, turned out to contain two inches of ice.

Only on March eighteenth did Kendrick and I finally put up the last of our buckets and do our first boiling. We made less than a gallon, though between us we had 102 buckets up.

The next few days were reasonable March weather, not warm enough for good sap runs, but warm enough to keep our hopes up. Then it went back to being cold again—zero on March twenty-sixth, eight above on the twenty-seventh. We didn't boil again until the twenty-ninth, and this time we made two gallons. I had bought a grading set (the so-called temporary kind that costs $3) the preceding week, while I was over getting cans at Grimm's. Naturally I tested what we had made so far, and to my amazed delight it came out Fancy grade. Some of that sap had been in the pans for two weeks.

The real season only began on March thirty-first, which is very late for central Vermont. On that day, for the second time ever, I had the wooden tank full to the brim: four barrels of sap, enough to make four gallons of syrup. And on April first we made, not four gallons—the prudent operator leaves a reserve of sap in the bottom of his tank for emergencies—but three and three-quarters. Grade A, and beautiful stuff. From then on we had enough sap to boil every other day. Ken and I took turns, so that each of us was actually at the sugarhouse one day in four. When the season ended on April fifteenth—the weather by now hot, the ground nearly bare, and sap turning cloudy in buckets—we had made three gallons of Fancy, seven of A, and a little over thirteen of B. Total: twenty-three gallons. We should have had more.

But prices were high this year, and each of us made a decent sum of money. After keeping a year's supply for ourselves, mostly in glass canning jars, and giving a certain amount to friends and relatives (ditto), we had sixteen gallons to sell. This we put in gleaming new cans. Not half-gallons, because we decided to sell outside the region, and other producers told us that city stores don't want half-gallons, only pints and quarts. So I had bought fifty pint cans for $14.50 and fifty quart cans for $16.50.

Most of the syrup we sold in New York City for $2.75 a quart and $1.50 a pint. (More for Fancy, less for B.) New Yorkers either have very small appetites or very small pantries, and the stores we sold to thought our cans were still too big. Next year we'll put some in half pints. After deducting $31.00 for cans and nothing for the trip to New York (I was going anyway), we had receipts of $162.75. Since I was providing the evaporator, the wood, and the greater part of the sap, we split this two-thirds to me and one-third to

Ken. Syrup for ourselves we split equally.

Next year will be bigger. I already have negotiations under way to buy more buckets—good used ones from Willis's Cousin Augustus, who has two thousand of them. If the deal goes through, his stock will drop to nineteen hundred. Between us Ken and I plan to hang at least a hundred and fifty next year and, if we can find enough accessible maples, possibly the whole two hundred the evaporator will handle.

We know by experience that supermarkets won't touch our product. I once wrote, proposing a syrup deal, to the manager of the A & P in the New York suburb where I grew up. He never answered. Instead I got an answer from the Bronx Buying Office of the A & P. A pleasant buyer explained that managers of million-dollar chain stores have no authority to buy anything. Only he and his colleagues could do that. So when I was in New York I went to see him, taking a pint of Grade A and my daughter Lily with me. He then further explained that he bought for 160 stores, and couldn't possibly be bothered with an order of less than 30 cases a week, and even then didn't think much of buying from individuals. The chain store is out. But next spring, if all goes well, a growing number of corner stores in New York will have a small lot of *new* direct from the producer.

POSTPOSTSCRIPT, 1986. Fifteen sugar seasons have come and gone since this book first appeared. Much has changed in the maple world—though I'm happy to say that there's even more that hasn't.

For big sugar operations, a lot of new technology has become available. The most conspicuous part of it is the reverse osmosis machine. That's an expensive device (up to $20,000) which uses membranes plus electricity plus complex laws of physics to remove water from unheated maple sap. It is not exciting to watch. There is no visible drama at all. Just lots of loud noise from the hidden motors inside. It's like watching a diesel locomotive when you are used to steam engines.

The comparison isn't exact, because diesels pull

trains on the entire trip, while reverse osmosis will not take sap all the way to syrup. Sooner or later even the biggest and most high-tech operators must turn off the electricity, fire up their evaporators, and do a little real sugaring. But it is close enough.

Noise and boringness are not the only problems with reverse osmosis. There are numerous people, me included, who think that syrup made with its help has inferior flavor compared to that produced entirely by boiling. For this reason, not to mention the initial expense, many big operators choose not to use it.

Small-scale operations have changed much less. In my own case, only one technical aspect is different. About nine years ago I finally entered the plastic age. I bought a thousand-foot coil of small tubing (it cost $49 at Grimm's), and put one grove of hard-to-get-at maples on pipeline. That means each tree has a couple of bright blue plastic spouts connected by pale lavender tubing. From the last tree, the tubing drops to the ground and runs downhill across a pasture, over a swamp, and so to my sugarhouse. On a good day, a slender stream of sap pours steadily from the end of the pipe into the holding tank.

The first year I put tubing up, I worried some that the four cows in the pasture would get to sniffing around and pull it loose from the trees, or maybe trample it where it crosses their paths. But they have never shown the faintest interest in all that lavender network (which seems a bit uncowlike of them), and my problems have been quite other. One is that the first couple of years, until I learned to store the tubing properly between seasons, mudwasps would come and build nests in almost every spur line. The tubing is 5/16″ in diameter, and apparently that dimension is a mudwasp's dream. Now I'm careful, after washing up, to pack the tubing away in tightly woven grainsacks.

The other problem is freezing. Lying directly on the snowy ground as it does, the pipeline tends to melt little canyons for itself, and hence to be in shadow. It will thus thaw out and start running a full hour later than buckets. But then, being an airtight system, it also runs later in the afternoon, and I think the yield per tap is nearly as high.

These days I have 30 pipeline taps, and depending on how ambitious I feel in a given year, somewhere between fifty and seventy-five buckets. Yields have been good. There was one extraordinary year when I made fifty-seven gallons of syrup from 104 taps—more than twice what the traditional quart-per-spout rule says one is entitled to expect. But even in a normal year my trees yield sap enough to make between twenty-five and thirty gallons of syrup. That much maple syrup contains about two hundred pounds of actual sugar. It pleases me to think that I have now made more sugar in my life than I have consumed.

Naturally there have been some smaller changes, too. Long ago I discovered that there was no need to be taking a little jar of cream down to the sugar-house every time I boiled. Now I take one pat of butter down on the day I first fire up. It lasts right through the season. A speck not much larger than a pinhead works nicely. Throw in a larger amount

—say, a piece the size of a small green pea cut in half—and you're in trouble. It will keep the pans from foaming up, all right, but it distinctly does not calm the boil. Surface tension is reduced so much that big gouts of boiling sap begin to leap in the air like dolphins. Soon they are leaping clear out of the pan and splashing onto the sugarhouse floor. Considering that this is partly boiled stuff, and considering that all of it (except what flows down the pipeline) I have painfully lugged from the trees by hand, I'm not about to see it wasted like that.

Another change is that I have learned to make maple candy, and I now own half a dozen molds. Two are antiques from the nineteenth century, in each of which I can make forty-eight tiny maple sugar hearts. The other four are modern ones, which produce large maple leaves, fir trees, maple men and women. My now-grown daughter Amy, no longer interested in gathering or boiling, still loves making the candy. Once she and her sister made several hundred little sugar hearts to be sold (to small children, for a penny each) at the village fair. They used less than a quart of syrup.

I have also changed markets and marketing techniques. New York was too far, and half-pints were too hard to pack. In a dark sugarhouse, you can't see inside those little metal cans. The spout is too narrow. No matter how much practice you have, they fill up faster than you think; and every fourth or fifth time, hot syrup comes flooding out the top.

These days, my basic container is the little 1.8 oz. glass bottle known in the trade as a nip. I fill them up at the house, seated comfortably at the kitchen table. You can see the level rise as you pour, and I have never yet had one run over. A friend who owns a printing business designed a label for me, and the little bottles look quite elegant. I sell them for sixty-five cents apiece to a bookstore in Boston— along with a few cans. There *are* city people who want quantity.

The last big change is in prices. Syrup has gone way up, and so has the equipment you make it with. If I were starting out now instead of in 1969, I would have to make a serious capital investment. The same little 2 × 6 evaporator that I bought for $340 now sells for about $1500. (It's true the pans are now made of stainless steel instead of tin, and they should last a lifetime.) Similarly, the three-barrel gathering tank that cost me $80 now sells for $370. My beautiful gathering pails, once a bargain at $9.00 each, now retail for $32.75. And so on.

There are some inexpensive new options, though. Grimm's has recently developed a 2' × 4' rig, with a thirty-three-inch flue pan and a fifteen-inch flat-bottomed syrup pan, which they sell for $790. Leader, the other big manufacturer of evaporators, up in St. Albans, Vermont, has a little 2' × 3' flat-bottomed rig for $395. I wouldn't consider either one if I wanted to make more than five to ten gallons of syrup a year, but for a really small producer I think they would work just fine.

As for syrup, demand has risen steadily over the past fifteen years—it's part of the natural foods movement—and prices have kept pace. In some city stores, they can be downright awesome. I happened to see a whole shelf full of Vermont maple syrup in a gift shop at Logan Airport in Boston this spring. The prices were not only high, but vulgarly stated. They were all in that penny-less-than-a-real-price style which assumes that we customers can't tell a false bargain from a true one and also know nothing about arithmetic. The Logan store wanted $13.99 for a quart, $9.99 for a pint, and $6.99 for a half-pint.

It was the half-pint price that drew an actual gasp from me. Eight ounces of syrup for $7.00. Back in 1970 I was selling half-gallons for $4.00—eight times as much syrup for just over half the price.

No sane person, of course, looks for bargains in airports, except maybe in duty-free shops, and even there I have my doubts. What I think of as normal prices in 1986 are more like $8.00 for a quart, $5.50 for a pint, and $3.50 for half a pint. At least that's about what they'd be in a country store in New England. They may rise a little, later this year, because the 1986 season was the worst in a couple of generations, and syrup will be in short supply. But they will probably come back down in 1987.

Just in case they don't, though, I think I'll probably hang an extra twenty buckets. It still seems to me that sugarers are producing something quite wonderful, maybe even a sacred article. But that doesn't mean they can't make a little money when a good year comes along.